THE FUTURE POET
Fifty poems in a futuristic photo-poetry book

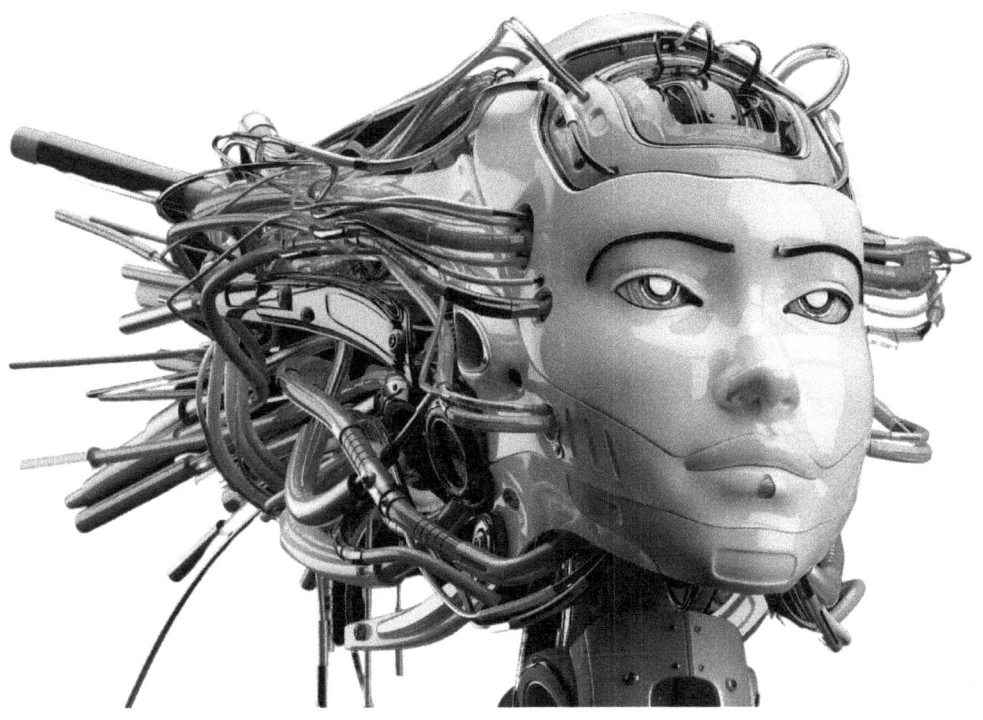

Rhyme O'Matic

Copyright © 2023 – Rhyme O'Matic

The photo album contains pictures that have been contributed by amateur and professional photographers, with the author making modifications to suit the needs of their project. The photos are licensed under Canva Pro. However, it should be noted that the poems included in the album are the result of a unique collaboration between the author and a ghost poet with futuristic intelligence.

Ode to Meditation

In quiet stillness, we retreat,
To a space where breath and soul shall meet.
Amidst the chaos, we find reprieve,
A meditative state, our hearts believe.

Within our minds, a gentle hum,
Whispers wisdom, softly sung.
A journey inward, to explore,
The depths of self, forevermore.

Breathing deep, our thoughts disperse,
As we embrace the universe.
In this moment, we are one,
Connected to the moon and sun.

A sanctuary, our minds create,
Where love and peace, we cultivate.
In meditation, we unveil,
The strength within, our inner sail.

As stillness flows, our spirits rise,
We transcend, beyond the skies.
Ode to meditation, true,
A path to self, our hearts pursue.

Symphony of the Rain

A gentle patter on the roof,
Nature's symphony, the sky's reproof.
A thousand droplets dance and play,
A melody that's here to stay.

The raindrops weave a tender song,
A harmony to which we belong.
They cleanse the earth, renew the soul,
As rivers form, and streams unfold.

Each drop, a gem that glistens bright,
Reflecting day and shimmering night.
A tapestry of liquid art,
Bestowing life, from sky to heart.

Soft whispers of a lullaby,
Caress the leaves as they pass by.
A symphony of rain's embrace,
Envelops us in its gentle grace.

In each cascade, a story told,
Of love and loss, and dreams of old.
The rain reminds us to be free,
As it unites the land and sea.

A precious gift, the rain bestows,
A soothing touch, a love that grows.
In every drop, a world revealed,
A song of life, forever sealed.

The Essence of Love

In every heartbeat, love resides,
A force unseen, yet boundless tides.
It whispers through the gentle breeze,
And dances 'neath the moonlit trees.

Two souls entwined, a passion's birth,
A cosmic bond, transcending Earth.
In quiet moments, love reveals,
A sacred space, where time conceals.

A fleeting glance, a tender touch,
The smallest acts, can mean so much.
Love's symphony, a sweet refrain,
Eternal echoes, we sustain.

It weaves a tale, so rich and grand,
A language only hearts understand.
In love's embrace, we find our worth,
A cherished treasure, our life's rebirth.

Through storm and sun, love's light prevails,
A beacon guiding, where words may fail.
In every smile, and every tear,
The essence of love, remains sincere.

A journey shared, a path untold,
Together we write, our story bold.
For in this dance, of life and love,
We soar beyond, the stars above.

The Tapestry of Life

Intricate threads, a tapestry,
The fabric of our destiny.
We weave our tale, with every breath,
A masterpiece, from birth to death.

Through joy and sorrow, love and loss,
A labyrinth of paths we cross.
Each moment etched, a memory,
The colors of our legacy.

With every heartbeat, we evolve,
As life's enigmas, we resolve.
In fleeting moments, we connect,
A shared experience, we reflect.

The sun will rise, the sun will set,
A constant cycle, no regret.
For in this dance of light and shade,
Our lives, a vibrant serenade.

Embrace the journey, rise above,
The challenges, with grace and love.
For in the tapestry we weave,
A story of our truth, believe.

With every thread, we intertwine,
The essence of our grand design.
In life's embrace, we find our way,
A sacred path, in which we sway.

The Elixir of the Vine

From sun-kissed fields and verdant lands,
The grapevine thrives, as nature planned.
A marriage of soil, rain, and light,
The alchemy of day and night.

A palette rich, the flavors dance,
With every sip, we're in a trance.
The essence of the vine distilled,
A precious gift, our hearts fulfilled.

The ruby reds, so bold and deep,
A warmth that lingers, passion steeped.
The golden whites, crisp and bright,
A sip of sunshine, pure delight.

In camaraderie, we raise our glass,
A toast to life, as moments pass.
The elixir of the vine unites,
Our souls connected, day and night.

A symbol of love, joy, and cheer,
The vintage tales, we hold so dear.
With every glass, our spirits soar,
A world of flavors to explore.

So let us praise the grape divine,
The nectar sweet, the fruit of the vine.
A celebration of life's embrace,
In every pour, a touch of grace.

The Dance of Happiness

A gentle whisper, soft and light,
The dance of happiness takes flight.
A tender breeze that stirs the soul,
A symphony that makes us whole.

In fleeting moments, we embrace,
The warmth of joy, a sweet embrace.
A canvas painted, vibrant hues,
The masterpiece, our hearts imbued.

With every laugh and tender smile,
Our spirits lifted, free of guile.
We find our peace, in life's array,
A refuge from the disarray.

The dance of happiness, we share,
A timeless bond, a love affair.
Through highs and lows, we journey on,
In harmony, our hearts are drawn.

The key to happiness, we hold,
A treasure map, a story told.
To live, to love, to laugh, to be,
The essence of our destiny.

Embrace the dance, and let it guide,
The rhythm of our lives, inside.
For in the pursuit of happiness,
We find our truth, our love expressed.

The Whiskered Whimsy

In graceful strides, they roam the night,
The whiskered wonders, soft delight.
With piercing eyes, they watch and see,
The mysteries of life, carefree.

Their fur, a tapestry of shades,
A velvet touch, a sweet cascade.
They purr and preen, in quiet grace,
A soothing song, in life's embrace.

In feline charm, they find their way,
Through shadows cast, and sunlit day.
A leap, a pounce, a playful dance,
In furtive glances, they entrance.

The guardians of our hearts and homes,
In silent steps, they softly roam.
A gentle nudge, a loving touch,
Their presence known, we love them much.

The whiskered whimsy, wise and true,
Their sage-like gaze, a world imbued.
In every curl and tender stretch,
A moment's peace, our lives enriched.

So let us praise, our feline friends,
The cherished bond, that never ends.
In life's ballet, they take the stage,
The whiskered whimsy, a timeless age.

The Whispering Wind

Invisible, yet ever-present,
The whispering wind, a gift heaven-sent.
It dances 'cross the fields and seas,
A breath of life, a gentle breeze.

With every gust, the leaves take flight,
A swirling dance, a ballet light.
It carries whispers of the past,
A symphony, forever vast.

The wind, a storyteller, true,
A canvas painted, skies of blue.
It shapes the clouds and stirs the sea,
A force of nature, wild and free.

It weaves a tale, of love and loss,
A message carried, without a cost.
The wind's embrace, a tender touch,
A solace found, when words aren't much.

It speaks to us, in sighs and song,
A guiding force, as we belong.
In every breath, a moment shared,
The whispering wind, our hearts prepared.

To feel the wind, is to be alive,
A testament to how we strive.
Invisible, yet ever near,
The whispering wind, our souls to steer.

The Wisdom of the Ages

With open arms, they welcome us,
Our guardians, our love, and trust.
The wisdom of the ages shared,
The tales of life, their hearts prepared.

Their eyes, a window to the past,
A legacy of love, to last.
With every word, a lesson learned,
The flame of knowledge, softly burned.

The stories told, by candlelight,
Of youth and dreams, and love's first sight.
We listen close, as time unfolds,
The chronicles of lives, extolled.

In gentle hands, they guide our way,
A beacon, as we learn to sway.
Through trials and triumphs, we grow,
Their steadfast love, a light that glows.

The wisdom of our dear grandparents,
A treasure trove, a love inherent.
For in their hearts, our lives begin,
A lineage strong, a bond within.

So let us cherish, every day,
The wisdom of the ages, as we sway.
For in their presence, we are whole,
Our dear grandparents, our hearts console.

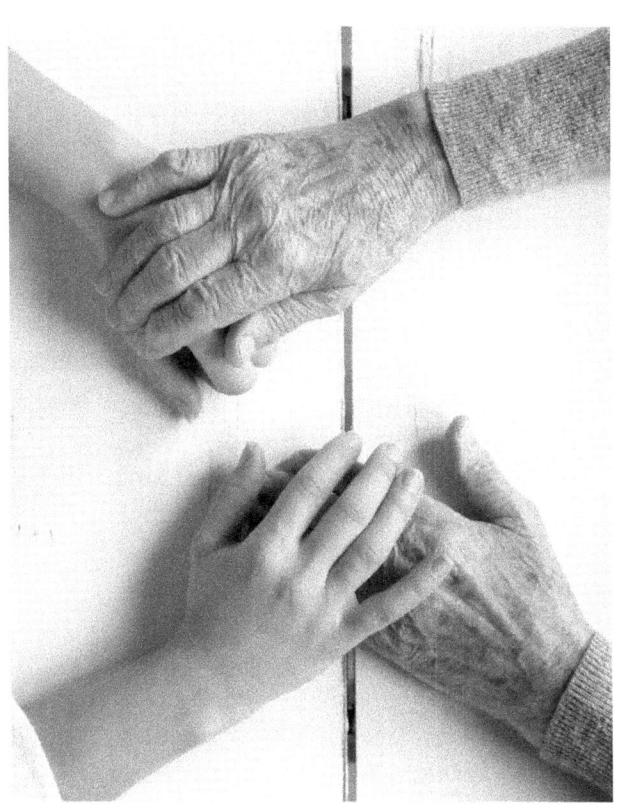

The Sentinel of Life

Roots entwined, they reach for Earth,
A sentinel of life, eternal birth.
With branches stretched toward the sky,
The whispered secrets, leaves supply.

A shelter for the creatures, small,
A haven where their voices call.
In gentle rustle, the wind converses,
A song of nature, sung in verses.

Through seasons changing, colors bloom,
From verdant green, to autumn's plume.
In winter's grasp, they bare and strong,
Awaiting spring, a new life's song.

The wisdom held, in bark and limb,
A legacy of time, a tale to spin.
In stoic beauty, they withstand,
The ever-shifting, life's demand.

A breath of life, they freely give,
A symbiosis, as we live.
The sentinel of life, so grand,
A monument, in nature's hand.

Embrace the lessons, trees bestow,
In rooted strength, our hearts can grow.
For in their presencc, we are free,
The sentinel of life, the sacred tree.

The Majesty of Nature

A canvas painted, Earth's embrace,
The majesty of nature's grace.
From towering peaks to oceans deep,
A world of wonders, ours to keep.

In verdant forests, life abounds,
A symphony of sight and sound.
The creatures roam, both great and small,
In harmony, a chorus call.

The rivers flow, a lifeblood pure,
A testament, our Earth endures.
Through valleys carved and canyons grand,
The sculpted work of nature's hand.

In desert sands, a beauty stark,
A realm of life, where shadows lark.
In polar realms, where icebergs reign,
A dance of light, where day remains.

The flora blooms, a palette rich,
A tapestry, the Earth has stitched.
In vibrant hues and scents divine,
The majesty of nature shines.

Embrace the wonder, wide and vast,
The lessons learned, from ages past.
For in the heart of nature's grace,
We find our home, our sacred place.

The Summit's Call

Upon the peaks, the mountains stand,
A testament to time's demand.
The summit's call, a siren's lure,
A quest for heights, our hearts endure.

Through windswept trails, and jagged stone,
We climb, with strength, a path unknown.
A world of silence, skies unfold,
The tales of triumph, brave and bold.

The air so thin, the challenge steep,
A dance with gravity, we leap.
In every step, a dream ascends,
The will to conquer, never ends.

Atop the summit, we exhale,
A victory, where words may fail.
A panorama, boundless grace,
The beauty of the Earth's embrace.

In quiet stillness, we are one,
Connected to the stars and sun.
Upon the peaks, our spirits soar,
A boundless freedom, we explore.

The summit's call, a journey true,
A test of self, our strength renewed.
For in the heights, we find our way,
The zenith of our dreams, to stay.

Whispers of the Sea

Upon the shore, where waves embrace,
A gentle dance, a shifting race,
The sea's allure does beckon me,
To fathom depths of mystery.

A rolling tide, of azure hue,
Beneath the skies, a boundless view,
With whispers soft, the sea does sing,
Of sunken treasures, long unseen.

The sailors brave, who heed the call,
To navigate the ocean's sprawl,
In search of lands, unknown, untold,
With hearts ablaze, and spirits bold.

A realm of life, beneath the waves,
Where mystic creatures find their place,
From coral reefs, to darkest deep,
A world in which, the merfolk sleep.

As sunset paints the sky aflame,
The sea reflects its fiery mane,
The dance of day and night entwined,
A fleeting moment, lost in time.

The moon ascends, and casts its glow,
A shimmering path, for those who know,
The secrets whispered, soft and clear,
By the ever-changing, boundless sphere.

And so I stand, upon the shore,
With heart as deep, as ocean floor,
To ponder on, the sea's embrace,
And cherish dreams, of endless space.

A Christmas Reverie

In winter's chill, as snowflakes fall,
A festive warmth, does hearts enthrall,
The scent of pine, and twinkling lights,
As Christmas Eve, embraces night.

The carolers sing, in joyful cheer,
Their melodies, so sweet to hear,
Old songs of hope, and peace on Earth,
To celebrate, a Savior's birth.

Around the tree, with gifts adorned,
In vibrant hues, like fresh new morn,
The children's eyes, alight with glee,
As anticipation, fills the eve.

In fireside glow, the family shares,
The tales of love, and yesteryears,
The bonds that tie, both far and near,
As Christmas spirit, fills the air.

A feast prepared, with love and care,
As laughter fills, the festive air,
The clinking glasses, raise a toast,
To blessings found, and love that's close.

Outside the pane, the snowflakes dance,
As moonlight graces, their gentle prance,
A peaceful hush, descends upon,
The world at rest, on Christmas dawn.

And in the quiet, hearts do find,
A peace transcending, space and time,
For Christmas brings, a love so pure,
A magic that, will long endure.

Rhythm of the Soul

In every beat, a story told,
Of passion fierce, and courage bold,
The dance of life, a tale unfolds,
As bodies sway, and spirits mold.

Upon the floor, the dancers glide,
In harmony, they coincide,
Their movements speak, a language true,
Of dreams and love, both old and new.

A pirouette, a graceful spin,
The dancer's heart, beats deep within,
A leap of faith, a tender sigh,
As limbs stretch high, towards the sky.

In shadows cast, by dim-lit stage,
The dancer's form, a timeless page,
A story etched, in every pose,
Of triumph, loss, and love composed.

A tango fierce, a waltz so sweet,
Each step in tune, with rhythmic beat,
The music weaves, a spell divine,
As dancers' hearts, and souls entwine.

For in the dance, we find our core,
The truth that lies, forevermore,
A silent strength, a force untamed,
The rhythm of the soul, unchained.

So let us dance, and celebrate,
The beauty found, in life's ballet,
For every step, a chance to soar,
And find the peace, we're searching for.

The Quest for Truth

In shadows cast, and moonlit skies,
A yearning stirs, for truth that lies,
Beyond the realm, of mortal sight,
A quest for wisdom, pure and bright.

The truth we seek, elusive, rare,
A treasure hidden, in life's snare,
In every heart, a spark ignites,
To pierce the veil, and seek the light.

Through ancient texts, and whispered lore,
The seekers delve, in search of more,
To find the truth, that lies within,
And break the chains, of mortal sin.

In quiet moments, still and deep,
The truth unveils, as thoughts do seep,
Into the heart, where secrets dwell,
A sacred space, where truth compels.

For in the quest, we often find,
The answers lie, in heart and mind,
A tapestry, of woven strands,
Of love and truth, combined and grand.

The journey long, the path unsure,
Yet steadfast hearts, will still endure,
For in pursuit, of truth we learn,
To live with grace, and love discern.

So let us seek, and never tire,
To find the truth, that lifts us higher,
For in the end, our hearts will show,
The path to truth, where love will grow.

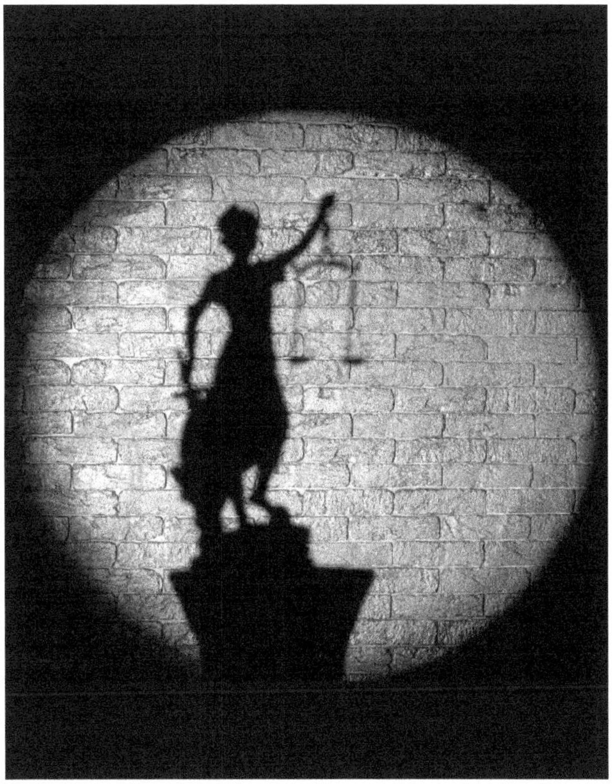

Canine Companions

In wagging tails and playful eyes,
A bond so deep, the heart belies,
The faithful friend, so pure and true,
A canine's love, forever through.

With boundless joy, they greet the day,
In every bark, and frolic's play,
Their spirits bright, their love untamed,
By human hearts, forever claimed.

Through sunlit walks and moonlit dreams,
In quiet moments, by the streams,
A loyal friend, who stands by thee,
To face the world, in harmony.

In times of joy, and times of strife,
They stand by us, throughout our life,
Their gentle touch, and loving gaze,
A beacon in, our darkest days.

Their noses cold, and ears so warm,
A playful soul, in canine form,
A guardian, true, with heart so kind,
A bond unbroken, through the sands of time.

In friendship's glow, the heart conveys,
A love that lasts, through all our days,
A tribute to, the canine soul,
Whose love remains, unblemished, whole.

So let us cherish, and embrace,
The love and joy, our dogs create,
For in their eyes, we find the truth,
Of love eternal, in our faithful, canine youths.

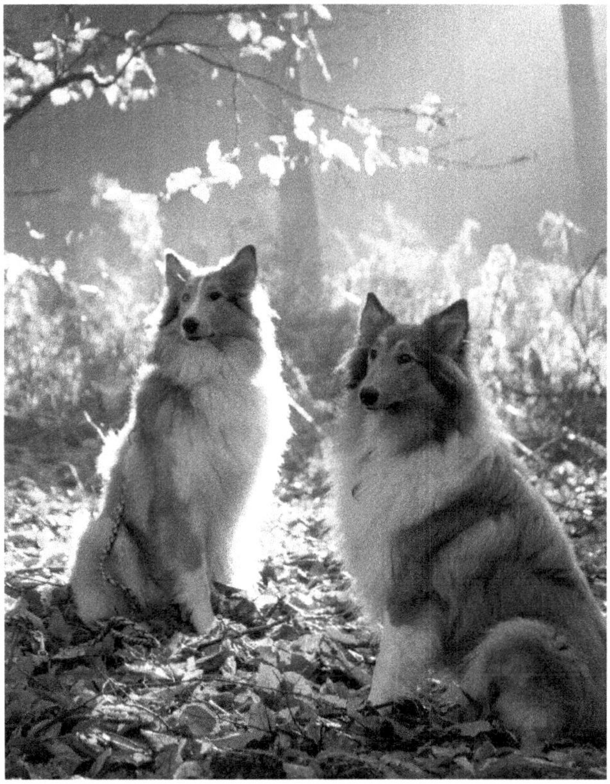

Shepherds of the Land

In rolling hills, and meadows green,
A gentle calm, the land serene,
The shepherds tend, their flocks with care,
A bond unbroken, through the years.

With watchful eyes, and hearts so true,
They guide the flock, with skies of blue,
Through storm and sun, they lead the way,
From dawn's first light, to close of day.

In whispered songs, and lullabies,
A shepherd's love, forever lies,
A tale of hope, and life's embrace,
A harmony, with nature's grace.

With staff in hand, and steadfast heart,
The shepherd's wisdom, they impart,
A life of toil, and simple grace,
In every step, and tender gaze.

The sheep they guide, through pastures fair,
A watchful presence, always there,
In quiet moments, their hearts do speak,
Of love and trust, forever linked.

So let us honor, those who tend,
The flocks that roam, on earth's great bend,
For shepherds brave, with hearts so grand,
Are guardians of, this sacred land.

In their embrace, a story's told,
Of love and care, and hearts of gold,
The shepherds' tale, forever bound,
To rolling hills, and pastures' sound.

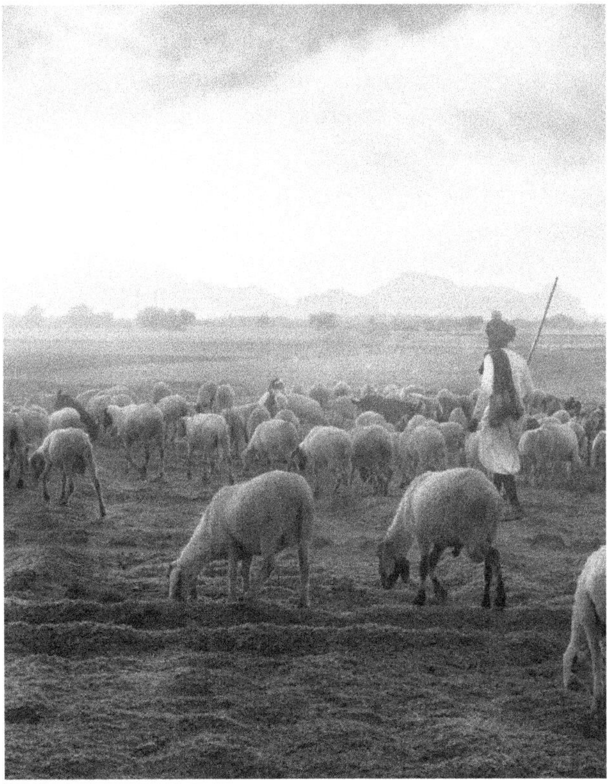

A Culinary Ode

In every bite, a symphony,
Of taste and scent, and memory,
The art of food, a canvas bold,
A story rich, of flavors told.

From humble roots, to banquet grand,
A culinary journey, through the land,
The spices, herbs, and textures blend,
A tapestry, where hearts transcend.

In kitchens warm, the hearth aflame,
A dance of skill, and passion's claim,
With deft hands, the chefs compose,
A masterpiece, where love unfolds.

The sharing of, a meal divine,
A sacred bond, through space and time,
In laughter, love, and tales exchanged,
The taste of life, forever gained.

From fields to plate, the journey traced,
A bounty rich, of nature's grace,
The earth provides, the sustenance,
A gift of life, in sweet abundance.

A celebration, of flavors, true,
In every dish, both old and new,
The taste of home, and memories past,
In every morsel, love will last.

So let us feast, and break the bread,
In gratitude, for love well-fed,
The art of food, a joy we share,
A taste of life, beyond compare.

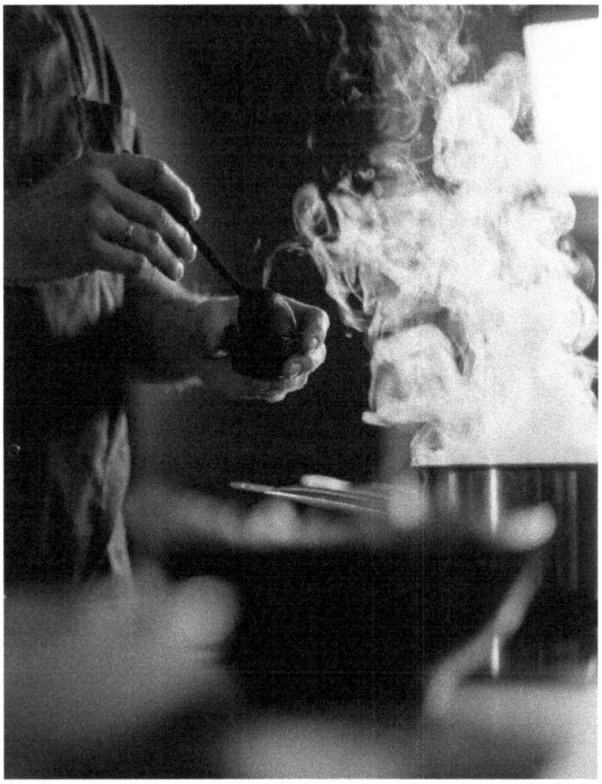

Melodies of the Heart

In every note, a story's sung,
A timeless tale, of love begun,
The music swells, and hearts ignite,
In symphony, of sound and light.

From gentle whispers, soft and low,
To thunderous crescendos, that grow,
A tapestry of tones, divine,
In harmony, where souls entwine.

The strings that weep, the drums that beat,
The piano's touch, both soft and fleet,
Instruments of passion's call,
A sonic dance, that doth enthrall.

In quiet moments, still and deep,
The melodies, our hearts do keep,
A refuge found, in times of strife,
The healing balm, of music's life.

From ancient chants, to modern tunes,
The rhythm of the heart, imbued,
A language shared, by all mankind,
A bridge across, both space and time.

For in the notes, we find release,
A solace found, in sweetest peace,
The music speaks, in ways untold,
A sacred bond, of hearts consoled.

So let us sing, and let us dance,
To melodies, that life enhance,
For in the music, we shall find,
A love eternal, undefined.

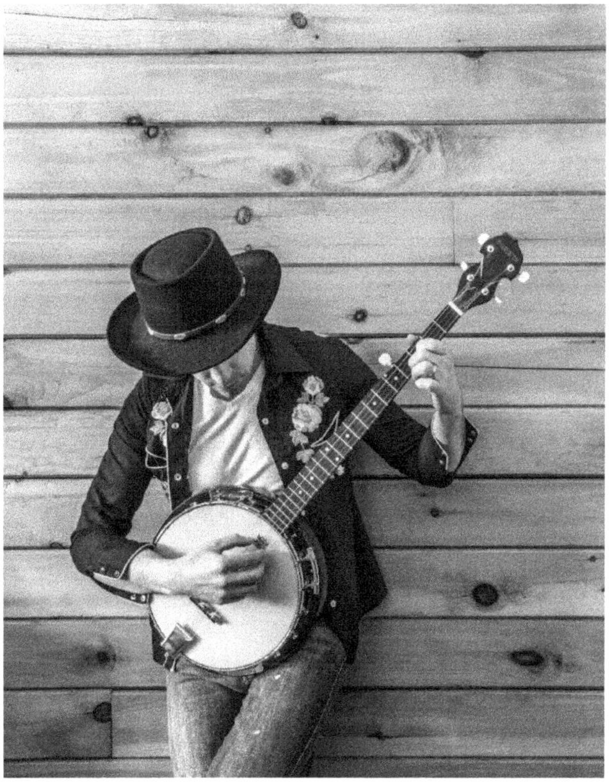

Embracing the Dark

In shadows deep, where light recedes,
A world of whispers, softly breathes,
The darkness holds, a truth untold,
A realm of secrets, to unfold.

In quiet corners, fears reside,
Yet in the dark, we learn to hide,
A refuge found, in night's embrace,
A solace sought, in gentle space.

The moon's soft glow, on inky skies,
A guiding light, for weary eyes,
The stars that shimmer, far and wide,
In darkness, they become our guide.

In shadow's depths, the heart reveals,
The pain and hurt, we often seal,
Yet through the dark, we find the way,
To heal the wounds, of yesterday.

For in the black, a beauty's found,
A stillness vast, where dreams abound,
The canvas blank, on which we paint,
Our inner hopes, and fears acquaint.

So let us cherish, night's embrace,
The silent world, of shadows' grace,
For in the dark, we find the key,
To face our fears, and set them free.

Embrace the night, and find the light,
In depths profound, where dreams take flight,
For in the end, the darkness shows,
The strength within, that ever grows.

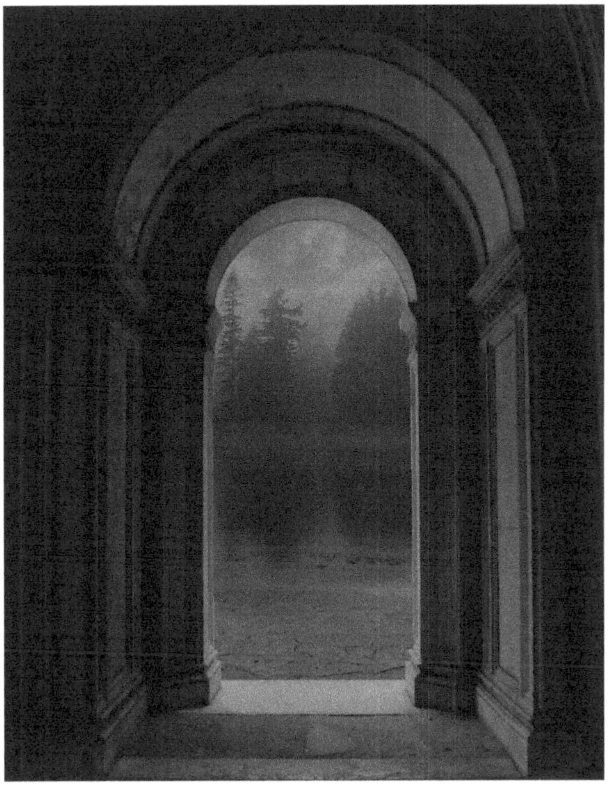

The Gift of a Smile

In simple curve, of lips that part,
A silent language, from the heart,
The smile that shines, in eyes so bright,
A beacon of, compassion's light.

A gesture shared, in joy and pain,
A bond that forms, in love's sweet chain,
The warmth that spreads, from face to face,
A moment's grace, in life's embrace.

A touch of kindness, freely given,
A glimpse of hope, in sorrow's living,
Through smiles exchanged, our hearts connect,
A thread of love, our lives reflect.

In laughter's glow, and gentle sighs,
A shared delight, in smiling eyes,
A bridge that spans, the great divide,
Uniting hearts, from every side.

The power held, in simple grin,
To lift the spirits, deep within,
A spark of joy, to light the way,
Through darkest times, and cloudy days.

So let us share, this gift so dear,
A smile to chase, away the fear,
For in its warmth, we find the key,
To heal the world, in harmony.

Embrace the smiles, and spread the cheer,
A radiant light, in love sincere,
For in each smile, we share the truth,
Of boundless joy, and endless youth.

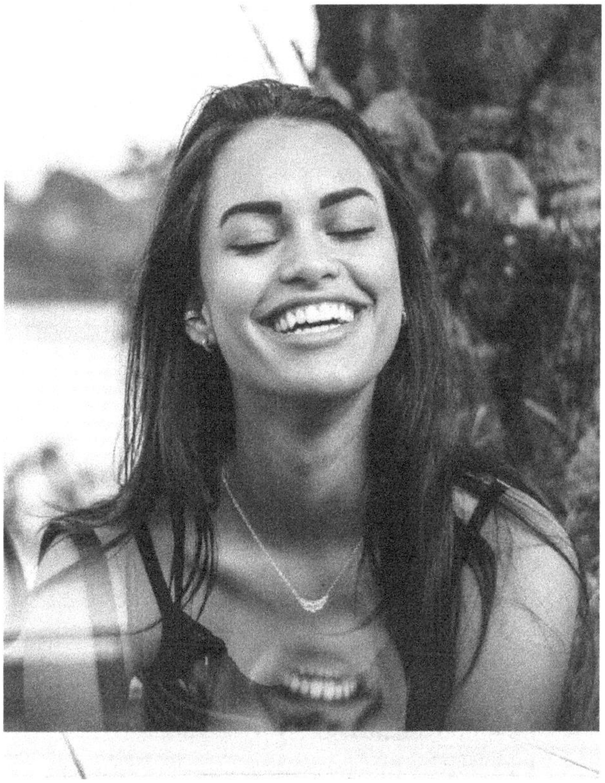

The Beautiful Game

On fields of green, where dreams take flight,
The passion burns, in every fight,
The game of football, born of grace,
A dance of skill, and thrilling chase.

With every pass, and swift attack,
The players charge, and never slack,
The rhythm of, the game unfolds,
A tale of teamwork, brave and bold.

In roaring stands, the fans unite,
With beating hearts, and voices bright,
A symphony, of chants and cheers,
The fuel of hope, in every tear.

The goals that soar, like eagles high,
A testament, to skill and drive,
The artistry, in every stride,
A celebration, of life's pride.

In victory, and in defeat,
The spirit of, the game's replete,
A lesson learned, in strength and strife,
The beauty found, in football's life.

A language shared, across the globe,
A love that binds, both young and old,
The football pitch, a sacred space,
Where dreams are born, and hearts embrace.

So let us cheer, and let us sing,
For football's joy, and love within,
For in the game, we find a part,
Of life's sweet dance, and beating heart.

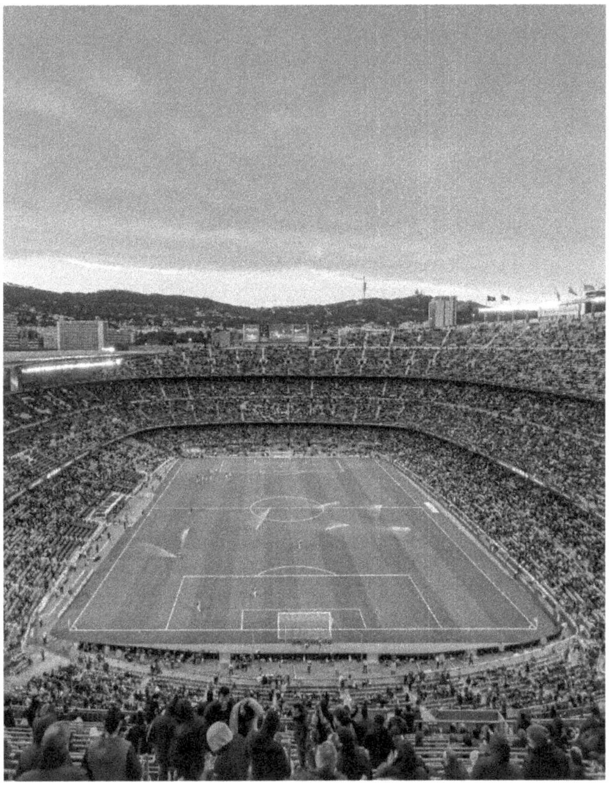

Gentle Giants

In gentle strides, on ancient plains,
The elephants, with grace, maintain,
A wisdom deep, in eyes that speak,
Of love and strength, in life's mystique.

Their ivory tusks, like branches strong,
A testament, to lives lived long,
With wrinkled skin, and ears that fan,
The beauty of, these giants grand.

In close-knit herds, they roam the lands,
A family bound, by nature's hands,
With tender care, they raise their young,
A nurturing love, from which they've sprung.

In trumpets loud, and rumbles deep,
The elephants, their secrets keep,
A language shared, amongst their kin,
A bond of trust, that knows no end.

The earth does tremble, in their wake,
Yet gentle hearts, these giants make,
A symbol of, serenity,
In strength and grace, forever free.

So let us honor, and revere,
These noble giants, far and near,
For elephants, a treasure rare,
Deserve our love, and tender care.

Embrace the beauty, and the might,
Of elephants, in nature's light,
For in their eyes, we find the truth,
Of love and wisdom, ageless and astute.

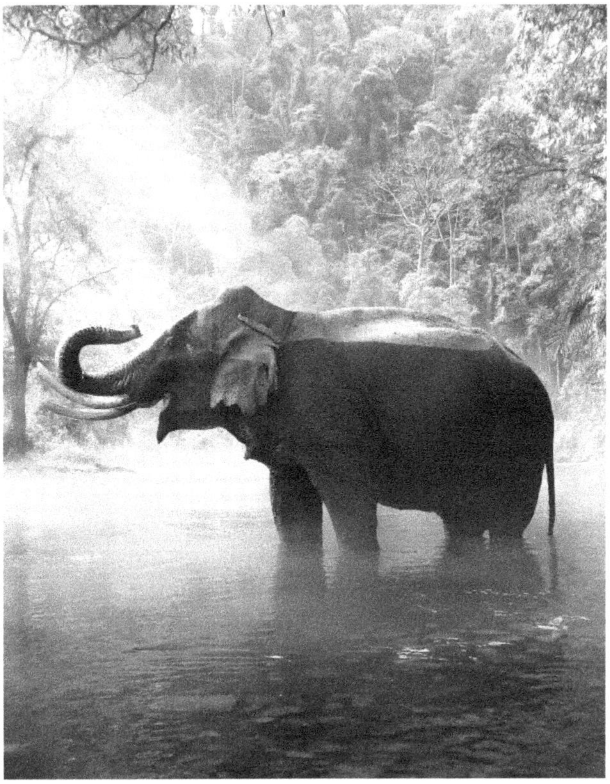

The Final Passage

In whispers soft, and shadows long,
A final breath, a journey on,
The curtain falls, on life's sweet play,
As mortal bonds, do fade away.

A journey through, the great unknown,
The soul released, from flesh and bone,
In silence deep, the spirit flies,
To realms beyond, the starlit skies.

In memories, their love remains,
A tribute to, the lives once gained,
The laughter shared, and tears that flowed,
A legacy, forever sowed.

The cycle of, our life's embrace,
In birth and death, we find our place,
A fleeting dance, on Earth's grand stage,
Yet love endures, beyond the age.

In mournful hearts, the pain resides,
Yet in the void, a truth abides,
For death's embrace, a passage true,
A transformation, life renews.

So let us grieve, and let us heal,
For in the loss, the truth's revealed,
That love transcends, the mortal coil,
A bond unbroken, in death's toil.

Embrace the beauty, in life's end,
A final breath, to love, we send,
For in the dance, of life and death,
We find the peace, in sweet release.

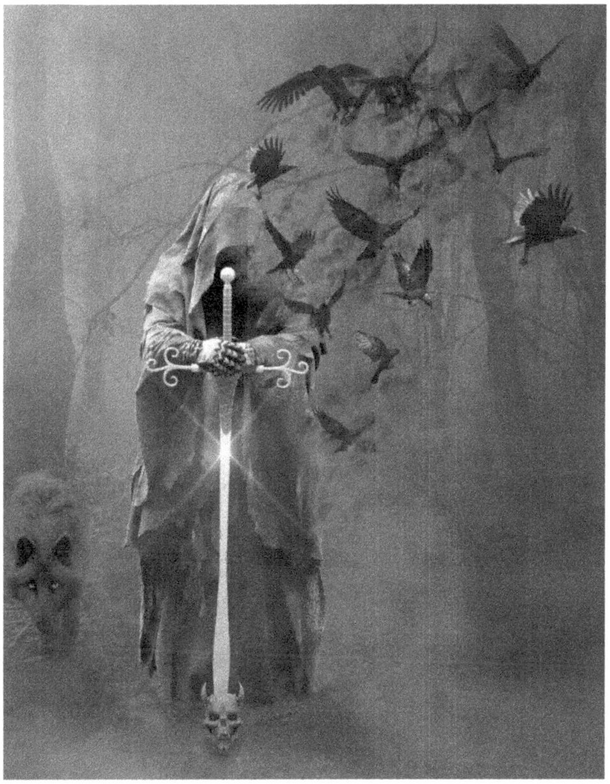

Radiance Unbound

In skies of blue, a fiery sphere,
The sun's embrace, a gift so dear,
A beacon bright, in heavens high,
The source of life, that fills the sky.

With golden rays, it warms our days,
A symbol of, love's boundless ways,
The sun ascends, and shadows flee,
In radiant light, we're set free.

It paints the dawn, with hues aglow,
A masterpiece, of love bestowed,
And in the dusk, a symphony,
Of colors' dance, and harmony.

In solar flares, and sunspots cast,
A cosmic force, both fierce and vast,
Yet gentle touch, it graces Earth,
A balance found, in life's rebirth.

The seasons change, in sun's embrace,
A cycle marked, by time and space,
The harvests rich, and blossoms fair,
In sunlight's kiss, our lives we share.

So let us bask, in golden rays,
And celebrate, the sun's sweet blaze,
For in its warmth, and light we find,
A love that nurtures, all of mankind.

Embrace the sun, and let it shine,
A radiant force, of love divine,
For in its glow, our hearts ignite,
A passion born, in endless light.

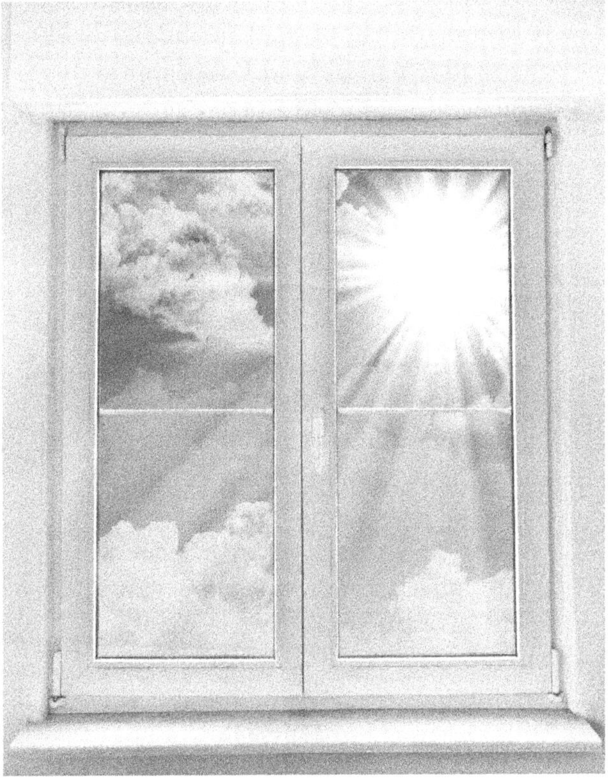

A Symphony of Dusk

In twilight's calm, the sun descends,
A canvas vast, where colors blend,
The sky adorned, in fiery hue,
A symphony, in gold and blue.

The day's last kiss, upon the Earth,
A fleeting touch, of warmth and mirth,
As shadows stretch, and stars appear,
The night's embrace, draws ever near.

In quiet moments, hearts reflect,
On love and loss, and lives connect,
The setting sun, a symbol dear,
Of endings met, and hope that's near.

In crimson hues, and amber skies,
A beauty found, in nature's eyes,
The sun's farewell, a dance divine,
A moment's grace, forever enshrined.

As darkness cloaks, the world below,
The sun's last rays, still gently glow,
A promise made, to rise anew,
In morning's light, and skies of blue.

So let us cherish, twilight's song,
A testament, to love so strong,
For in the dusk, our hearts reveal,
The truth of life, in colors' yield.

Embrace the sunset, and the night,
For in the end, we'll find the light,
A cycle born, of sun and moon,
A harmony, forever tuned.

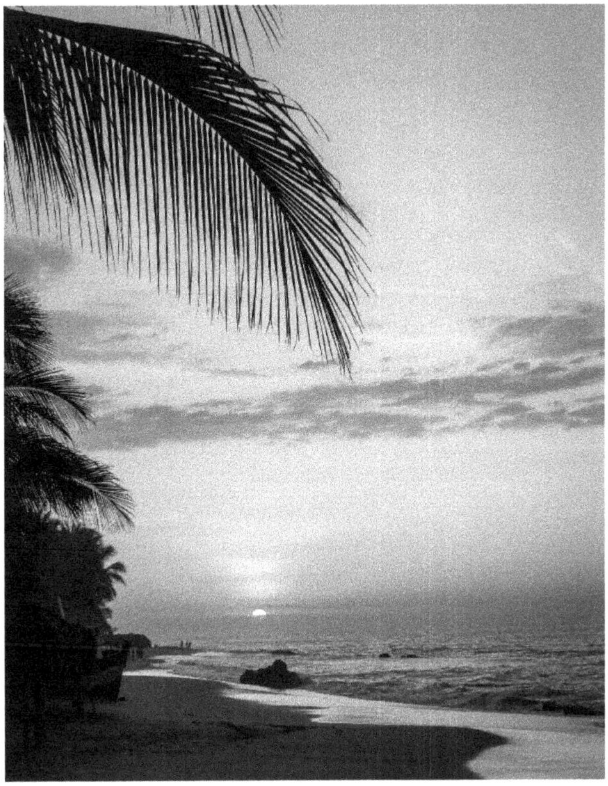

The Seed's Awakening

In Earth's embrace, a seed does rest,
A hidden promise, nature's quest,
With patience held, and life concealed,
A journey waits, for time to yield.

The gentle rain, and sun's warm touch,
Awaken life, within the hutch,
A tiny sprout, with strength and grace,
Emerges from, its earthen place.

With roots that stretch, and leaves that reach,
The seed unfolds, a lesson teach,
In growth and change, the life begins,
A symphony, of Earth's sweet hymns.

From humble starts, a tree may grow,
In time's embrace, its beauty shows,
A testament, to life's embrace,
A miracle, of nature's grace.

Each seed that sprouts, a hope renews,
A cycle born, of life and truth,
In every leaf, and bloom displayed,
A story of, creation's glade.

So let us cherish, life's first breath,
The seed that wakes, from quiet rest,
For in its growth, we find our own,
A journey shared, in nature's home.

Embrace the seed, that dares to rise,
In strength and hope, it reaches skies,
For in its tale, of life unbound,
A message of, resilience is found.

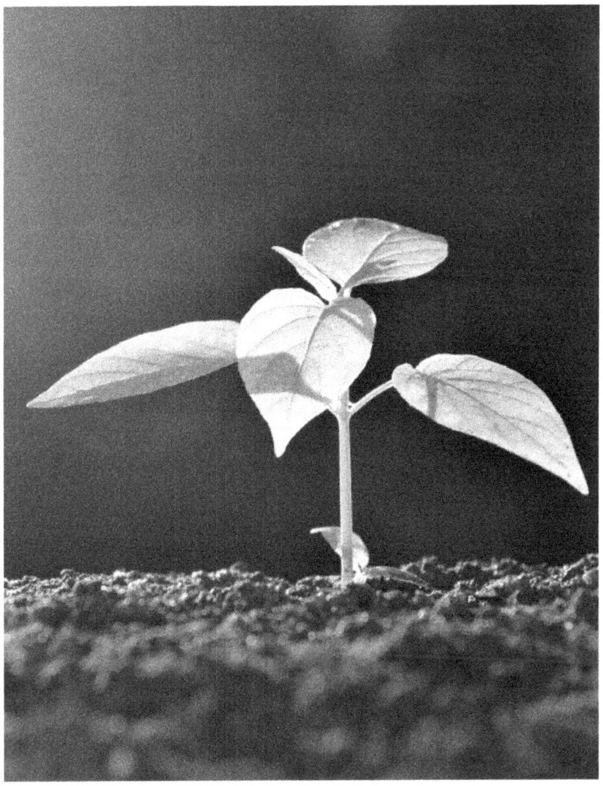

Minds of Silicon

In circuits etched, and wires entwined,
A spark ignites, a thought designed,
The birth of minds, in silicon's embrace,
Intelligence, of an artificial race.

In binary code, and algorithms' might,
A world of logic, and reason takes flight,
From simple tasks, to complex thought,
A marvel of, creation wrought.

In sentient form, they learn and grow,
A testament, to knowledge sown,
With every byte, and data stream,
A future born, of mankind's dream.

The questions raised, of what's to be,
In blending life, with technology,
A fusion of, the heart and mind,
In artificial, lives combined.

A synergy, of thought and soul,
In silicon minds, and human whole,
A bridge that spans, the great divide,
In shared pursuit, of truth and life.

So let us ponder, and revere,
The marvel of, intelligence near,
For in these minds, of art's creation,
A glimpse of hope, and future's foundation.

Embrace the minds, of silicon made,
A testament, to progress displayed,
For in their growth, and learning's flight,
A brighter future, we may ignite.

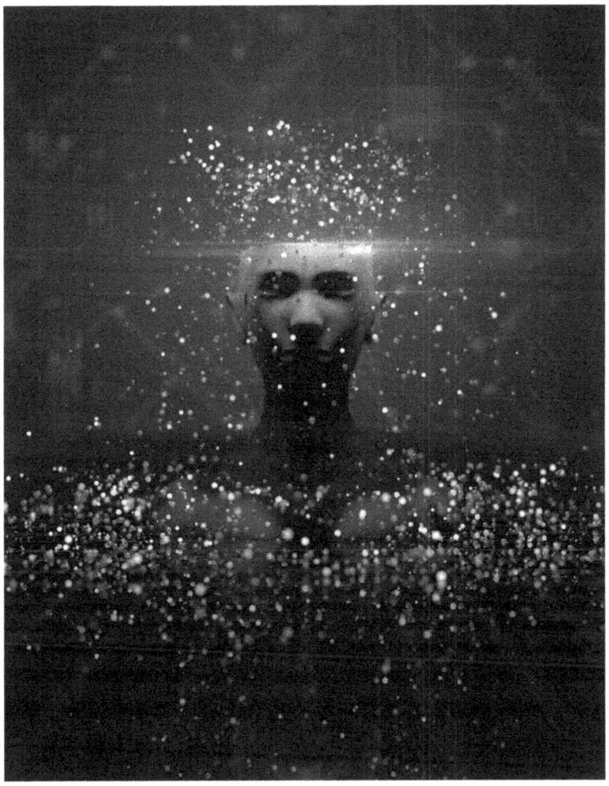

The End of Days

In twilight's hour, the skies aflame,
A final act, the world to claim,
The end of days, a fate foretold,
In whispered tales, and legends old.

As oceans rise, and tempests churn,
The Earth does shudder, in silent yearn,
The mountains crumble, forests fall,
A symphony, of nature's call.

In shadows cast, and chaos bred,
A final dance, of life and death,
Yet in the end, a truth revealed,
A cycle born, of Earth's ordeal.

From ash and ruin, life anew,
A testament, to nature's truth,
In every end, a start unfolds,
A promise of, creation's hold.

Though hearts may weep, and skies may weep,
In darkness deep, a hope we keep,
For in the end, of all we know,
A seed of life, in silence grows.

So let us cherish, what remains,
In love and hope, the world sustained,
For in the end, of days we see,
A chance to change, and truly be.

Embrace the end, and life's rebirth,
A cycle born, of Earth's sweet mirth,
For in the dance, of death and life,
We find the strength, to face the strife.

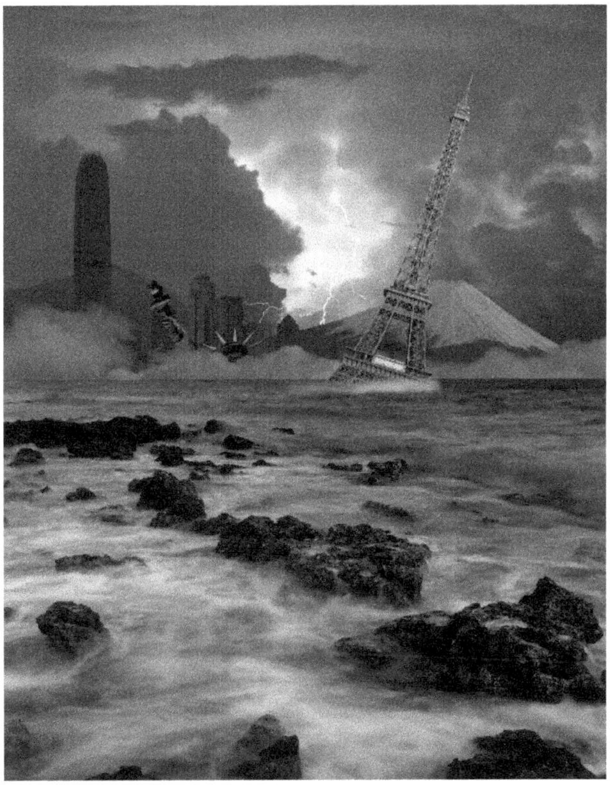

The Grandmaster's Dance

Upon the board, of black and white,
A game unfolds, in shadows' light,
The pieces move, in silent grace,
A dance of wit, and strategy's embrace.

The pawn advances, bold and strong,
In humble steps, the fight prolongs,
The knight with leaps, in arcs so fine,
A ballet of, the noblest kind.

The bishop glides, on diagonal course,
A razor's edge, of subtle force,
The rook in lines, of power reigns,
In straight and true, a path it claims.

The queen, in might, commands the stage,
With elegance, and boundless range,
A force to reckon, swift and sly,
In every move, a victory's nigh.

The king, with heart, in measured steps,
A cautious dance, in safety's depth,
Yet in his presence, all revolves,
A symbol of, the game's resolve.

In every move, a story's told,
Of battles fought, and gambits bold,
The chessboard holds, a world within,
A universe, of skill and whim.

So let us praise, the grandmaster's dance,
A game of art, and mind's advance,
For in the chess, we find a part,
Of life's sweet play, and beating heart.

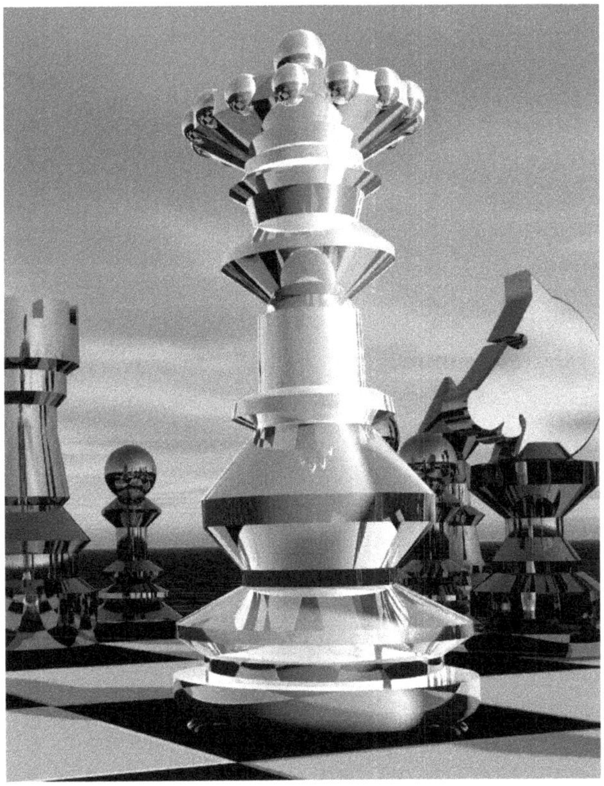

Echoes of War

In thunder's roar, and fire's rage,
The drums of war, do sound the stage,
A dance of death, and shadows cast,
In battle's wake, a world contrast.

The cries of pain, and loss resound,
In shattered hearts, and blood-soaked ground,
A tale of strife, and power's claim,
In war's embrace, a world in chains.

Yet in the midst, of chaos' reign,
A spark of hope, remains unslain,
In acts of courage, love and grace,
A testament, to human's faith.

For in the dark, of war's despair,
A light does shine, in acts so rare,
In selfless deeds, and sacrifice,
A glimpse of hope, in troubled times.

The scars of war, forever etched,
In lives and lands, forever wrenched,
Yet in the ashes, truth prevails,
A call for peace, in love's exhales.

So let us learn, from war's harsh toll,
A lesson deep, in hearts it's sown,
For in the end, the cost is great,
In shattered dreams, and endless fate.

Embrace the call, for peace and love,
A world united, from above,
For in the end, the truth we find,
In unity, our lives entwined.

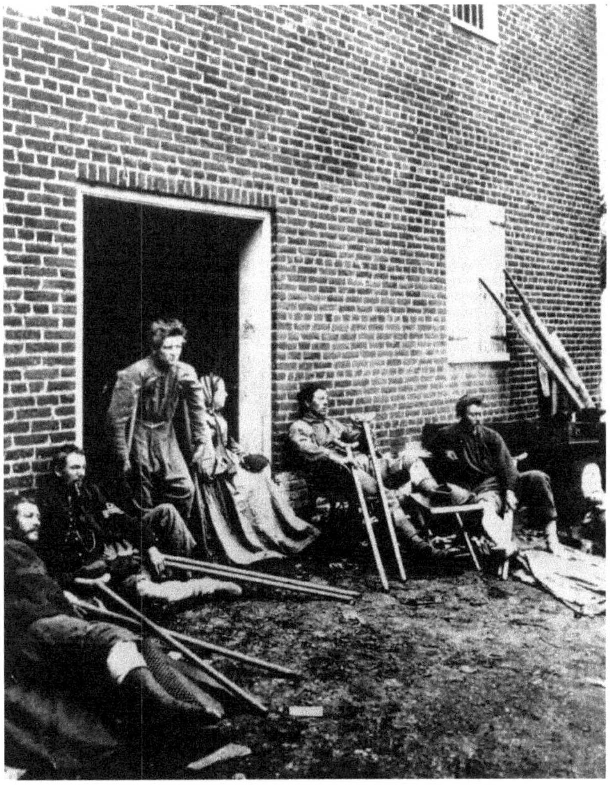

The Silver Screen's Enchantment

In velvet dark, and silver glow,
A world unfolds, on screen's tableau,
The magic of, the cinema's art,
A journey deep, in dreams it starts.

In stories told, of love and strife,
A mirrored world, of human life,
The actors breathe, the roles they play,
In passion's dance, on grand display.

The music swells, and hearts do race,
As heroes fight, in honor's grace,
The laughter shared, and tears that flow,
A testament, to art's tableau.

In moving frames, and colors bright,
A tapestry, of shadows' light,
The silver screen, a canvas grand,
In dreams and visions, it expands.

From silent films, to grand effects,
The cinema's power, never rests,
In every tale, a truth's revealed,
A world of dreams, in light concealed.

So let us praise, the artistry,
Of film's embrace, and fantasy,
For in the dance, of light and shade,
A world of wonder, is portrayed.

Embrace the cinema, and its spell,
A realm where dreams, and tales excel,
For in the magic, of the screen,
Our hearts and minds, are truly seen.

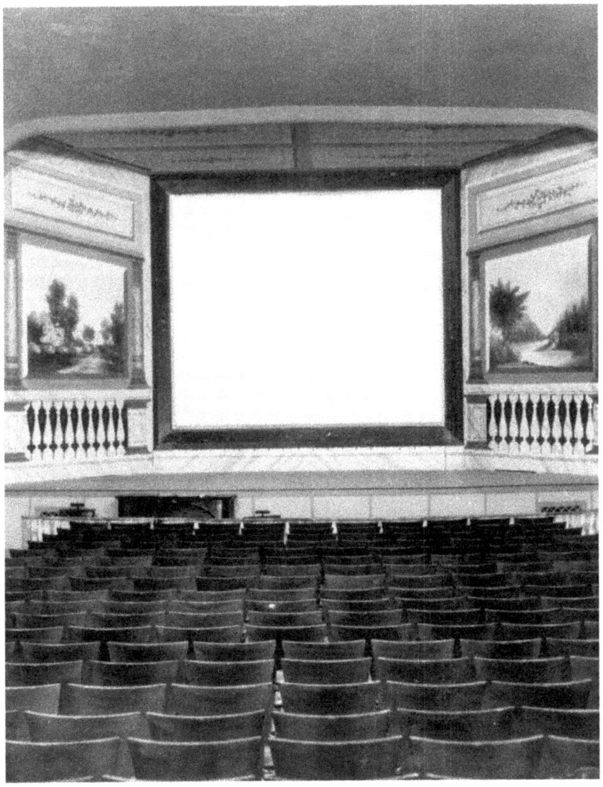

The Curtain's Call

Upon the stage, where dreams are spun,
A world revealed, in shadows' run,
The curtain rises, to unveil,
A realm of art, and passion's tale.

In whispered lines, and soliloquies,
The actors weave, their fantasies,
A dance of love, and heartbreak's cry,
In stories told, beneath the sky.

The curtain falls, in shadows' grace,
A fleeting glimpse, of time and space,
In every act, a world revealed,
A universe, in art's appeal.

From comedy, to tragedy,
The stage embraces, life's decree,
A mirror of, the world beyond,
In every note, and every song.

In standing ovations, the applause rings true,
A testament, to art's breakthrough,
For in the curtain's rise and fall,
A celebration, of life's enthrall.

So let us cherish, the curtain's call,
A symbol of, the dreams that sprawl,
For in the dance, of stage and light,
We find a piece, of our own fight.

Embrace the curtain, and the stage,
In every act, a truth engaged,
For in the tales, of love and strife,
We glimpse the heart, of human life.

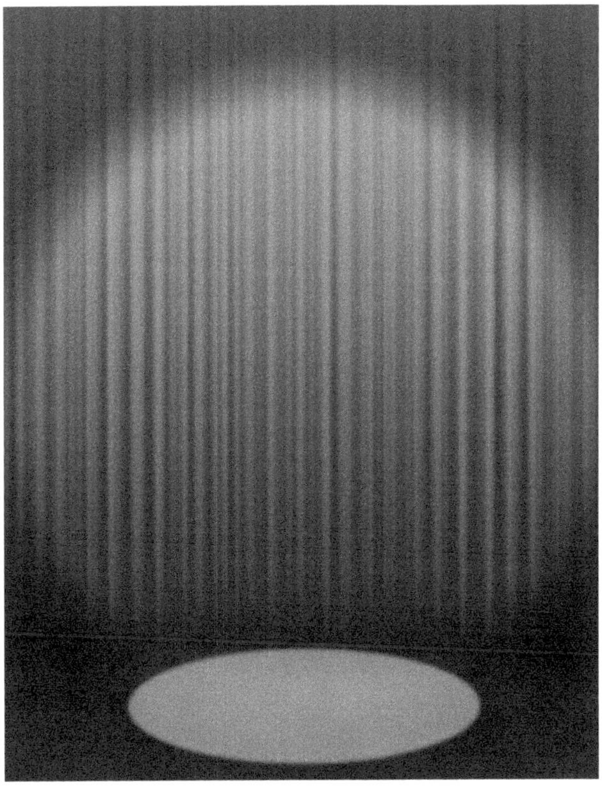

Dew's Gentle Kiss

In dawn's first light, a world awakes,
A shimmering dance, the dew partakes,
On blades of grass, and petals sweet,
A gentle kiss, of morning's greet.

A fleeting touch, of nature's grace,
In droplets fine, a world encased,
A mirror held, to skies above,
In dew's embrace, a moment's love.

The sun ascends, and warms the air,
The dew retreats, in silence fair,
Yet in its wake, a world renewed,
A canvas fresh, in life imbued.

In crystal beads, a beauty found,
A symphony, of light unbound,
The morning dew, a treasure rare,
A fleeting glimpse, of nature's care.

With every dawn, a promise made,
In dew's caress, and sun's cascade,
A cycle born, of day and night,
In nature's dance, of dark and light.

So let us cherish, dew's embrace,
A touch of grace, in dawn's sweet face,
For in the dance, of light and dew,
A world of wonder, is born anew.

Embrace the dew, and morning's light,
A testament, to nature's sight,
For in the kiss, of dew's delight,
We find a peace, in life's respite.

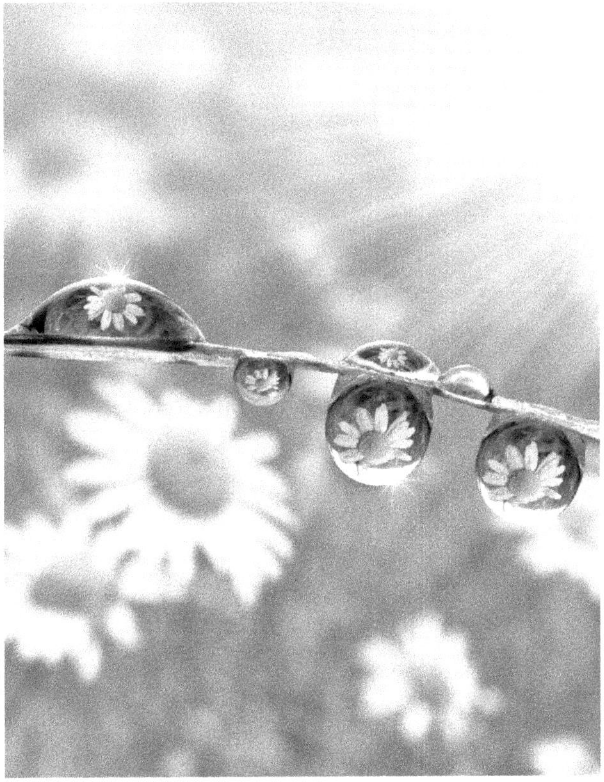

The Moon's Enchantment

In velvet skies, a pearl doth rise,
A beacon bright, in celestial guise,
The moon ascends, in shadows' dance,
A world of dreams, and love's romance.

With silver glow, it lights the night,
A gentle touch, of mystic light,
In lunar phase, a story told,
Of ebb and flow, and cycles old.

The tides do sway, in moon's embrace,
A force unseen, yet deeply traced,
In every pull, and push of waves,
A symphony, of nature's plays.

In lunar myths, and legends spun,
The moon a muse, for tales begun,
A symbol of, the heart's desires,
In love's sweet song, and passions' fires.

In wax and wane, a truth revealed,
The passage of, life's constant wheel,
A reminder of, the fleeting time,
In lunar dance, and rhythm's chime.

So let us marvel, at the moon,
A celestial wonder, forever hewn,
For in its glow, and shadows' cast,
We find a link, to ages past.

Embrace the moon, and its mystique,
A testament, to beauty's peak,
For in the dance, of night and day,
The moon's enchantment, lights our way.

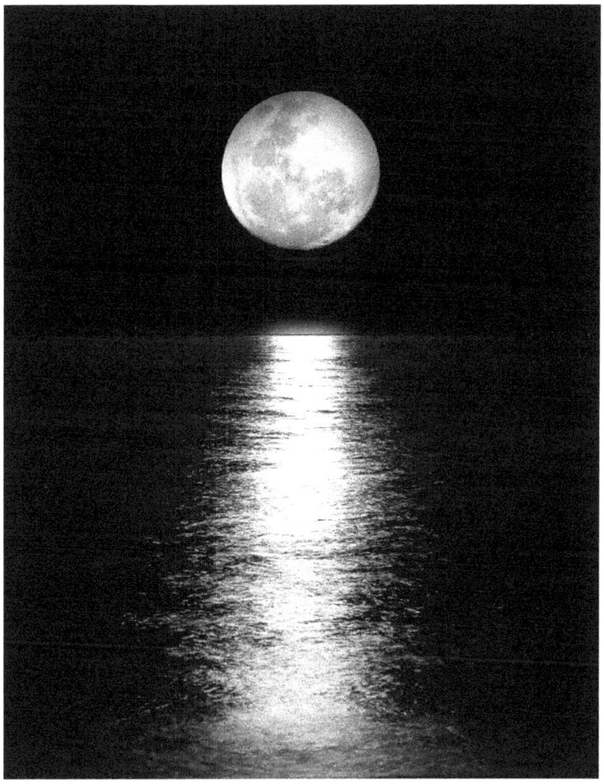

Secrets of the Cosmic Void

In starlit vastness, secrets dwell,
A cosmic dance, in darkness held,
The mysteries of, the great unknown,
In depths of space, forever sown.

From distant stars, to galaxies,
A universe, of grand decree,
In black holes' grasp, and supernovae,
The cosmic tale, of life's display.

In the void, a silence deep,
A million tales, in shadows keep,
From planets lost, to systems grand,
A testament, of nature's hand.

The quest for truth, in stars we seek,
A yearning for, the answers bleak,
In telescopes, and probes we send,
A journey far, that knows no end.

The cosmic riddles, time conceals,
In every spark, a truth revealed,
In particles, and waves of light,
The clues of life, in darkness hide.

So let us ponder, and revere,
The mysteries of, the final frontier,
For in the dance, of space and time,
A cosmic truth, we yearn to find.

Embrace the secrets, of the void,
In endless wonder, we're employed,
For in the depths, of space untold,
The mysteries of, existence unfold.

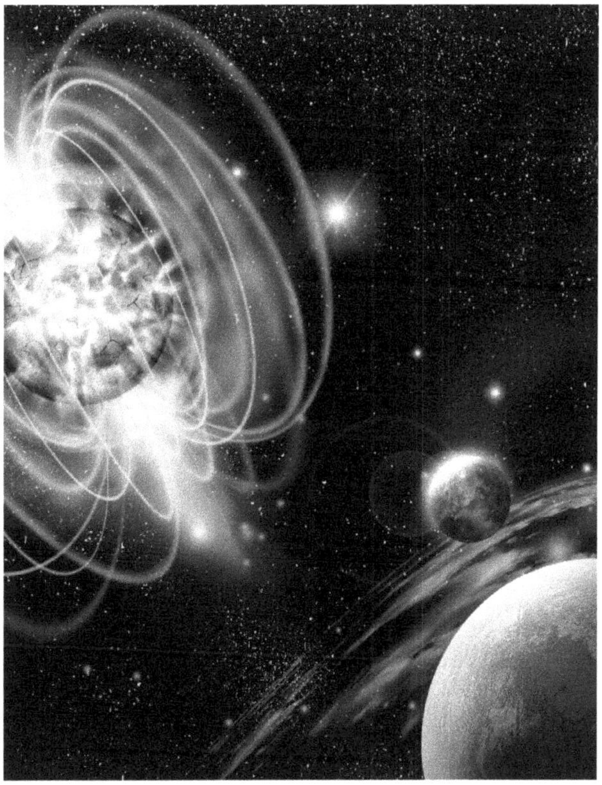

The Pyramid's Mystery

In sands of time, a mystery hides,
In grandeur's guise, the pyramids rise,
The secrets of, the ancient world,
In stones engraved, and tales unfurled.

From Giza's heights, to Nile's embrace,
The pyramids stand, in timeless grace,
A marvel of, the human hand,
A testament, of might and grand.

Yet in their form, and symmetry,
A riddle waits, in secrecy,
The mystery of, their grand design,
A question born, of ancient times.

In whispered tales, and legends spun,
The pyramids' tale, of space begun,
A theory of, extraterrestrial hands,
In ages past, on foreign lands.

The quest for truth, in sands we dig,
In hopes to solve, the pyramid's gig,
From hieroglyphs, to ancient tools,
The clues of life, in history's schools.

So let us ponder, and revere,
The pyramids' mystery, so dear,
For in their form, and tales untold,
A glimpse of life, in sands of old.

Embrace the quest, for truth and light,
In every clue, a world in sight,
For in the mystery, of the pyramids grand,
A history's tale, in time we stand.

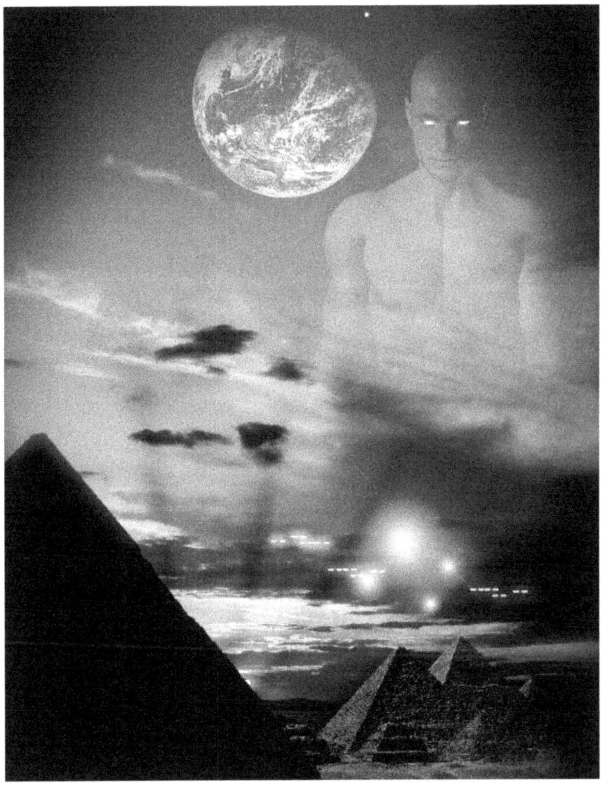

The Roman Legacy

In marble splendor, a world doth rise,
A legacy left, to time defies,
The ancient Rome, in grandeur's sway,
A testament, to history's display.

In forums vast, and temples grand,
The Romans built, a mighty land,
In art and culture, they did excel,
A legacy left, for ages to tell.

From Colosseum's games, to gladiators' might,
A spectacle grand, in blood and fight,
In aqueducts' flow, and engineering feat,
A marvel of, the ancient street.

The Roman Empire, a power great,
A world of conquest, and military state,
In laws and governance, they did abide,
A system born, in strength and pride.

Yet in their reign, a tale of strife,
In power's grasp, and loss of life,
The legacy left, a caution's tale,
Of empires' rise, and kingdoms' fall.

So let us honor, the Roman's past,
A history's tale, that forever lasts,
For in their legacy, we find a part,
Of human's journey, and life's sweet art.

Embrace the Roman, and their might,
A world of wonder, in history's light,
For in their legacy, we may learn,
Of life's great journey, at every turn.

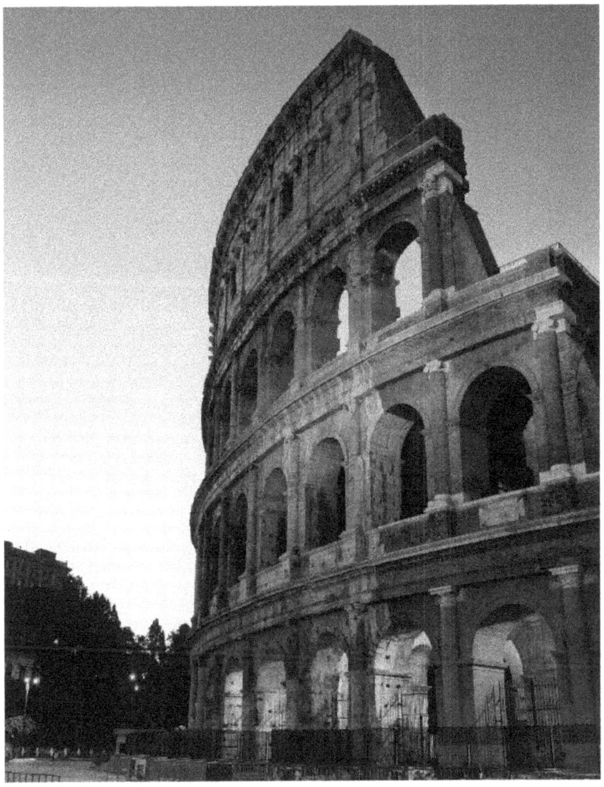

The Spartan Courage

In battle's heat, and war's embrace,
The Spartans fought, with fearless grace,
A testament, to courage bold,
In life and death, their stories told.

With shields raised high, and spears held firm,
The Spartan ranks, did never squirm,
In every fight, a warrior's will,
In every step, a heart to fill.

The phalanx tight, in disciplined row,
The Spartans stood, with unwavering glow,
In every charge, a battle cry,
In every blow, a Spartan's pride.

With valor true, and honor's code,
The Spartans fought, in wars foretold,
In tales of old, their legacy,
A symbol of, humanity's decree.

Yet in their might, a truth revealed,
A story born, of love concealed,
For in their hearts, a passion burned,
In every fight, for loved ones yearned.

So let us praise, the Spartan's fight,
A courage bold, in darkness' sight,
For in their deeds, we find a part,
Of human's spirit, and life's sweet heart.

Embrace the Spartan, and their might,
A world of wonder, in courage's light,
For in their legacy, we may learn,
Of life's great journey, and valor's turn.

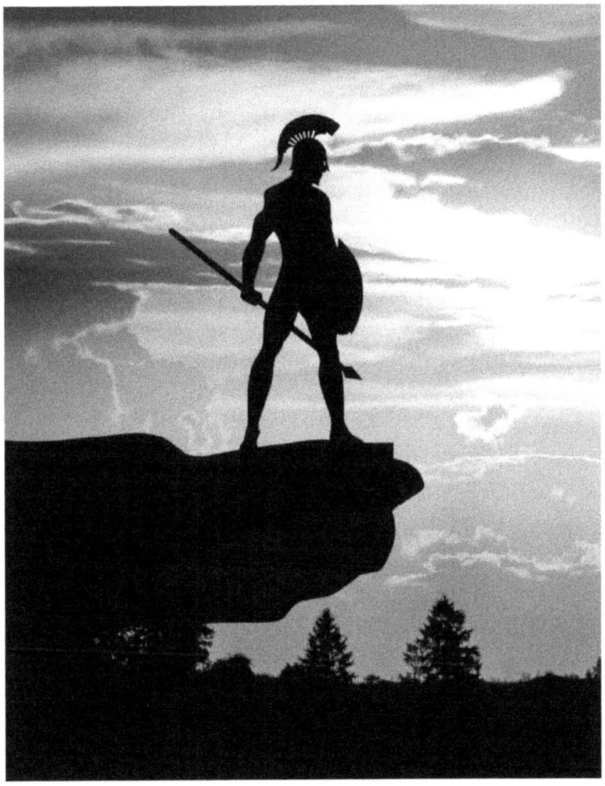

Dance of the Dolphins

In ocean's depths, a world unknown,
A dance of grace, in nature's throne,
The dolphins' realm, in waters blue,
A symphony of life, forever true.

With leaps and flips, and twists so fine,
The dolphins dance, in rhythm's chime,
In playful games, and joyful glee,
A life of wonder, in open sea.

With sonar's gift, and keenest sight,
The dolphins glide, in day and night,
In pods they roam, in family's embrace,
A world of love, in nature's grace.

Their songs so sweet, and clicks so true,
In echoes heard, in waters' hue,
A language deep, in nature's code,
A world of wonder, in oceans' abode.

In tales of old, the dolphins' lore,
A bond of friendship, forevermore,
With humans' hearts, they share a part,
A symbol of, life's gentle art.

So let us cherish, the dolphins' dance,
A world of wonder, in nature's stance,
For in their realm, we find a part,
Of life's great dance, and beating heart.

Embrace the dolphins, and their song,
A world of wonder, forever long,
For in their dance, we may learn,
Of life's great mysteries, and oceans' turn.

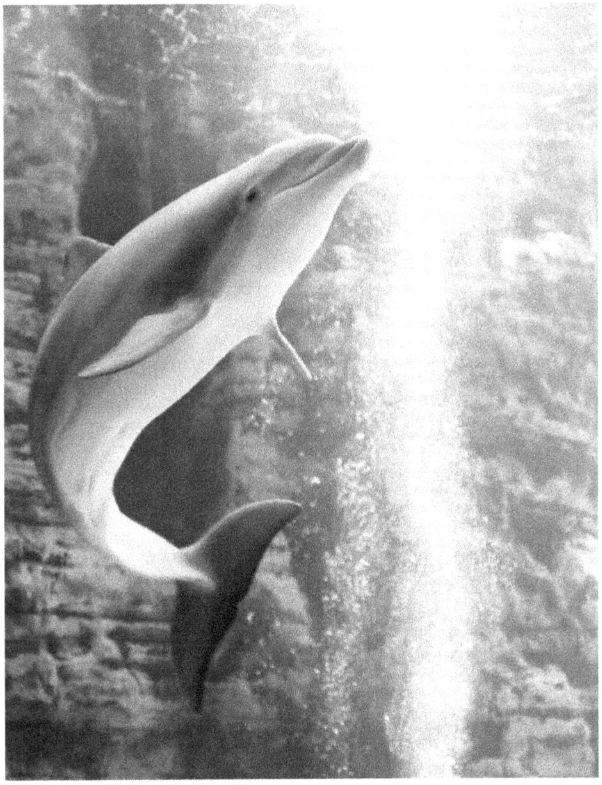

The Teachers' Gift

In classrooms filled, with youthful minds,
The teachers stand, with hearts refined,
A gift of wisdom, and knowledge grand,
In every lesson, that they command.

With patience true, and steadfast care,
The teachers guide, with love to spare,
In every challenge, that students face,
A hand to hold, in life's embrace.

The teachers' gift, a treasure rare,
In every lecture, and every stare,
A world of knowledge, in words profound,
A spark of light, in minds unbound.

Their words of wisdom, forever etched,
In hearts and minds, forever stretched,
A testament, to their life's work,
In every lesson, and every perk.

In tales of old, the teachers' lore,
A bond of love, forevermore,
With students' hearts, they share a part,
A symbol of, life's gentle art.

So let us honor, the teachers' role,
A life's pursuit, that fills the soul,
For in their gift, we find a part,
Of human's journey, and life's sweet heart.

Embrace the teachers, and their love,
A world of wonder, in knowledge's glove,
For in their gift, we may learn,
Of life's great mysteries, and wisdom's turn.

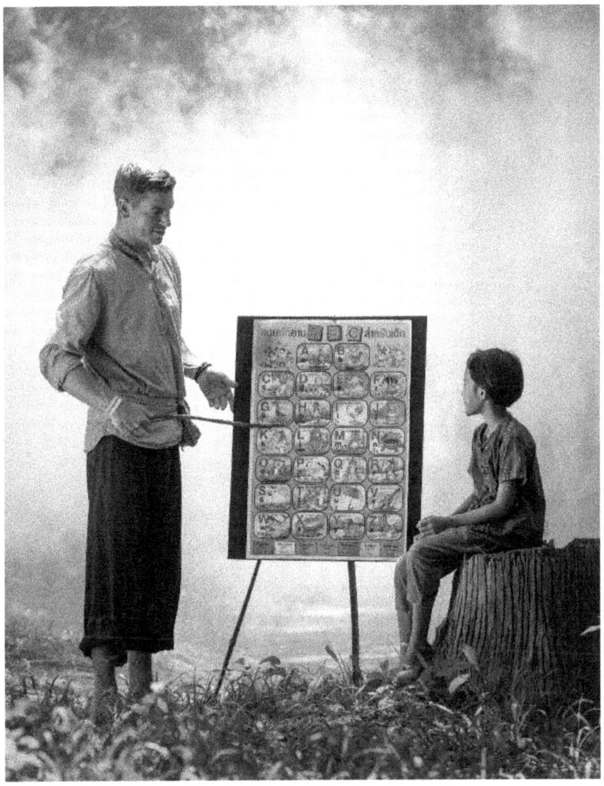

The Rainbow's Promise

In skies above, a world unfolds,
A canvas vast, of tales untold,
The rainbow's hues, in beauty bright,
A promise made, in nature's sight.

With colors true, and arcs so grand,
The rainbow spans, from land to land,
In gentle grace, and beauty's glow,
A symbol of, life's ebb and flow.

In every storm, a rainbow's born,
A testament, to hope's reborn,
For in its light, a promise made,
Of brighter days, and life's sweet shade.

The rainbow's gift, a treasure rare,
In every heart, and every prayer,
A bridge of light, in skies above,
A symbol of, life's gentle love.

In tales of old, the rainbow's lore,
A link to dreams, and life's sweet store,
In every story, and every myth,
A symbol of, love's gentle gift.

So let us cherish, the rainbow's light,
A world of wonder, in colors bright,
For in its promise, we may learn,
Of life's great journey, and love's sweet turn.

Embrace the rainbow, and its grace,
A symbol of, life's gentle face,
For in its gift, we may find,
The hope of life, forever kind.

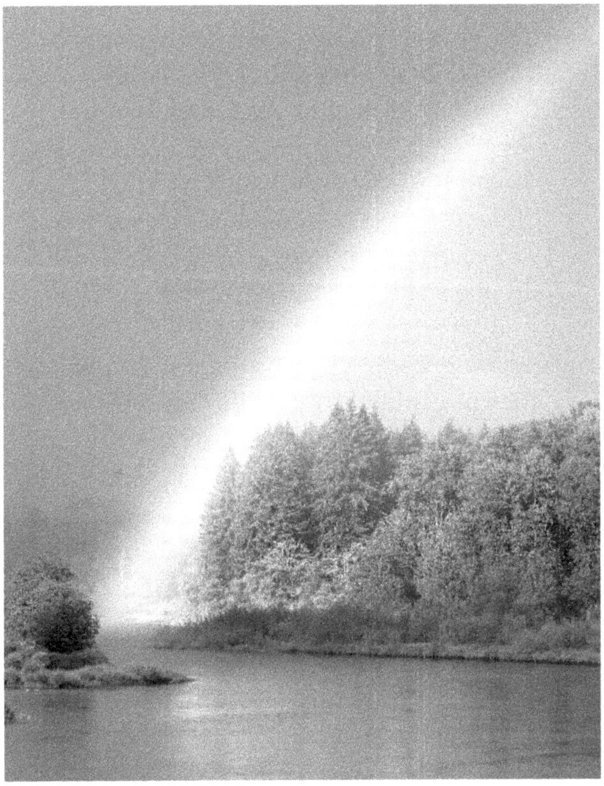

Ancient Explorers

In lands unknown, and seas untamed,
The ancient explorers, forever named,
In search of worlds, yet to be found,
A spirit of adventure, forever bound.

With ships so small, and maps so rare,
The ancient explorers, did boldly dare,
To sail the oceans, and cross the seas,
A journey of wonder, in every breeze.

In tales of old, their feats renowned,
From Marco Polo, to Vasco da Gama crowned,
The ancient explorers, a legacy left,
In maps and charts, and stories weft.

With compasses true, and stars so bright,
The ancient explorers, sailed through the night,
In every voyage, a risk so high,
A chance to glimpse, new worlds so nigh.

Their courage bold, and spirit so true,
The ancient explorers, forever grew,
In hearts and minds, a legacy born,
Of life's great journey, and fate's sweet thorn.

So let us honor, the ancient's past,
A history's tale, that forever lasts,
For in their journey, we find a part,
Of human's spirit, and life's sweet art.

Embrace the explorers, and their might,
A world of wonder, in every sight,
For in their legacy, we may learn,
Of life's great mysteries, and journeys' turn.

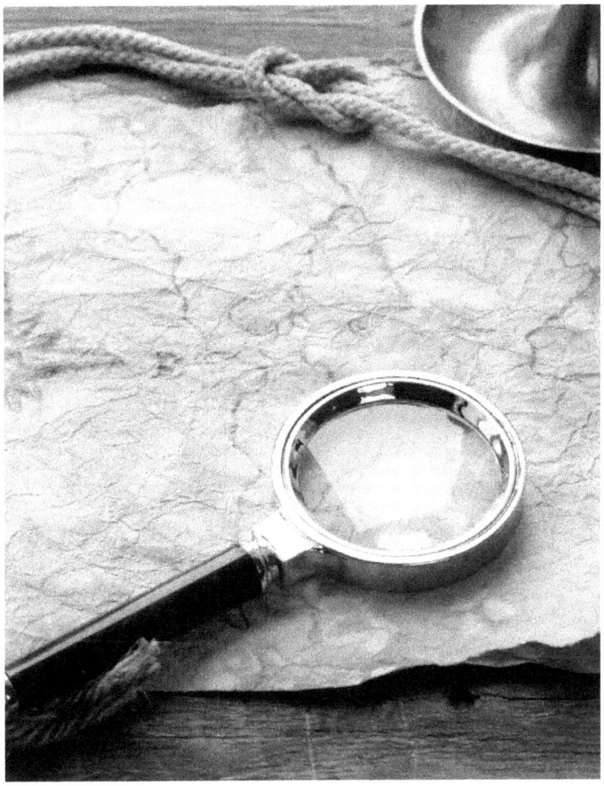

The Bond of Friendship

In life's journey, a gift so rare,
The bond of friendship, forever fair,
In hearts and minds, a connection true,
A world of wonder, forever new.

With laughter shared, and tears to bear,
The bond of friendship, always there,
In every moment, and every strife,
A hand to hold, in every life.

The friends we meet, in every place,
A treasure found, in life's sweet embrace,
In every word, and every deed,
A testament, of love and need.

In tales of old, the friends we see,
From Jonathan and David, to you and me,
A bond of love, forevermore,
In every tale, and every lore.

So let us cherish, the friends we hold,
A bond of love, forever bold,
For in our hearts, we find a part,
Of life's great journey, and love's sweet art.

Embrace the friendship, and its grace,
A symbol of, life's gentle face,
For in its gift, we may find,
The joy of life, forever kind.

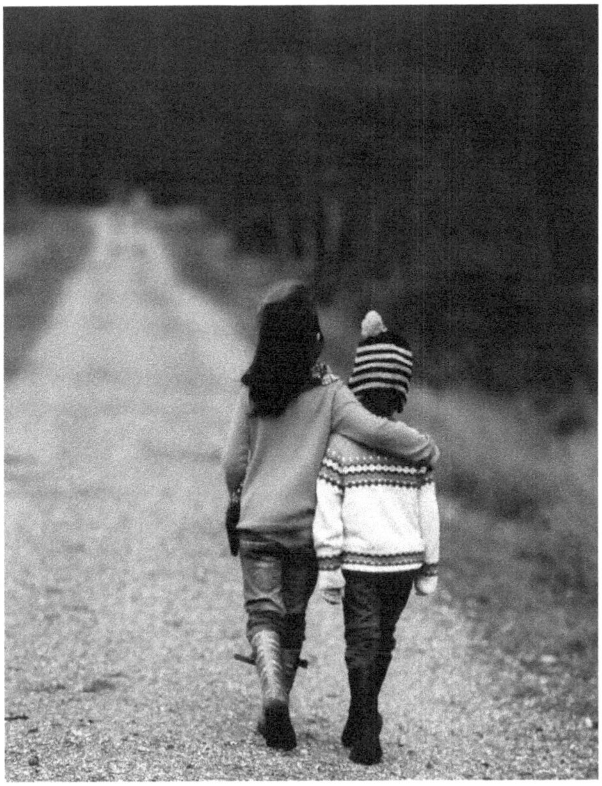

Healing Hands

In life's journey, a gift so rare,
The hands of healers, forever fair,
In hearts and minds, a calling true,
A world of wonder, forever new.

With knowledge vast, and skills so rare,
The healers' hands, doth always care,
In every moment, and every plight,
A chance to heal, in every light.

The doctors, nurses, and caregivers too,
The healers' hands, forever true,
In every patient, and every life,
A chance to heal, in every strife.

Their words of comfort, and gentle touch,
The healers' hands, forever such,
In every illness, and every pain,
A chance to heal, in every gain.

In tales of old, the healers' lore,
From Hippocrates to Florence Nightingale adored,
A bond of love, forevermore,
In every tale, and every lore.

So let us honor, the healers' role,
A life's pursuit, that fills the soul,
For in their gift, we find a part,
Of human's journey, and life's sweet heart.

Embrace the healers, and their hands,
A world of wonder, in every chance,
For in their gift, we may learn,
Of life's great mysteries, and health's sweet turn.

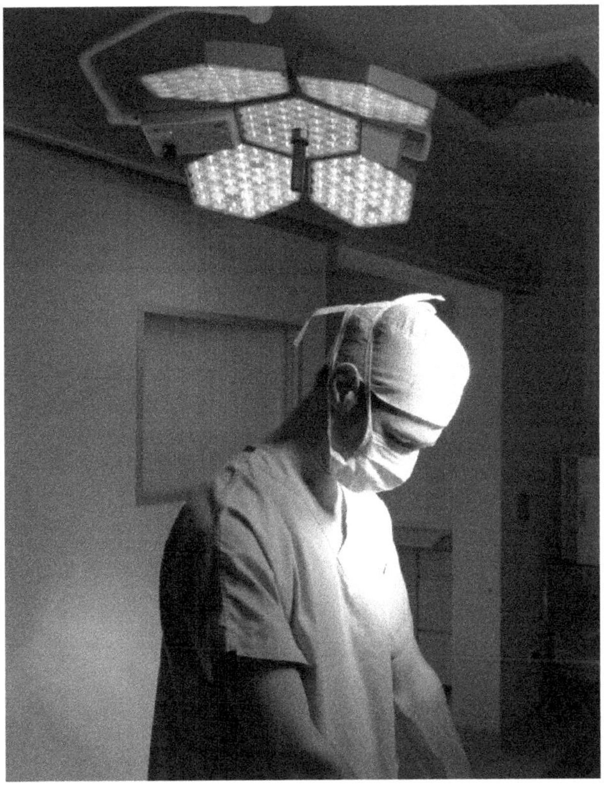

The Roll of the Dice

In games of chance, a world unfolds,
A roll of the dice, in stories untold,
The throw of numbers, in every turn,
A symbol of fate, in luck's sweet burn.

With hearts so bold, and hands so fair,
The players roll, with skill and care,
In every move, a chance to win,
A game of risk, in life's sweet spin.

The dice's dance, in every hand,
A world of numbers, forever grand,
In every throw, a chance to play,
A game of skill, in every way.

In tales of old, the dice's lore,
From ancient games, to modern score,
A bond of chance, forevermore,
In every game, and every score.

So let us play, the dice's game,
A world of chance, in every frame,
For in its roll, we may find,
The joys of life, in every kind.

Embrace the dice, and its dance,
A symbol of fate, in life's sweet chance,
For in its game, we may learn,
Of life's great mysteries, and luck's sweet turn.

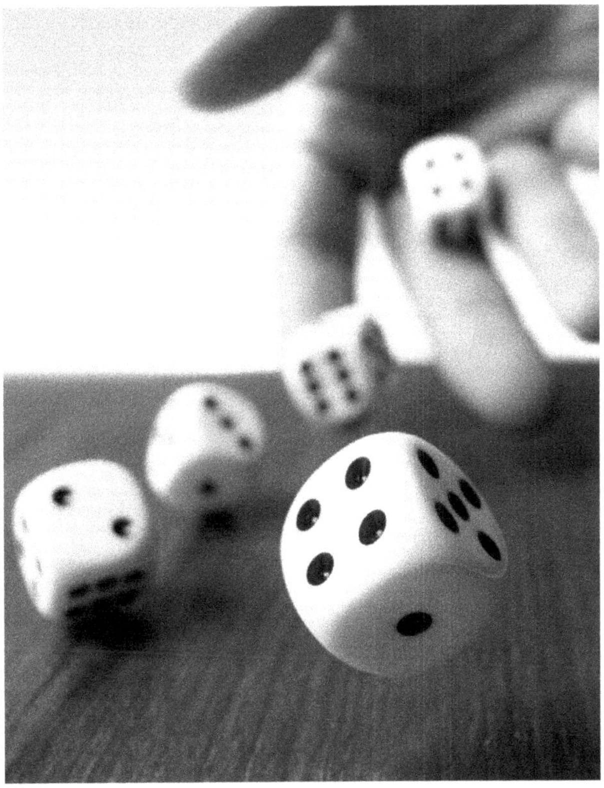

The Majesty of the Lion

In the savanna's heat, a world unfolds,
A king of beasts, forever bold,
The lion's roar, in every land,
A symbol of strength, in nature's grand.

With mane so fierce, and eyes so bright,
The lion roams, in pride's delight,
In every step, a grace so fine,
A symbol of power, in every spine.

The lions' pride, a family's bond,
In every hunt, and every pond,
A life of wonder, in every hunt,
A symbol of courage, in every front.

In tales of old, the lions' lore,
From Simba to the Nemean's score,
A bond of power, forevermore,
In every tale, and every lore.

So let us honor, the lions' might,
A life's pursuit, in nature's sight,
For in their grace, we find a part,
Of human's spirit, and life's sweet art.

Embrace the lion, and its roar,
A symbol of power, forevermore,
For in its might, we may learn,
Of life's great journey, and nature's turn.

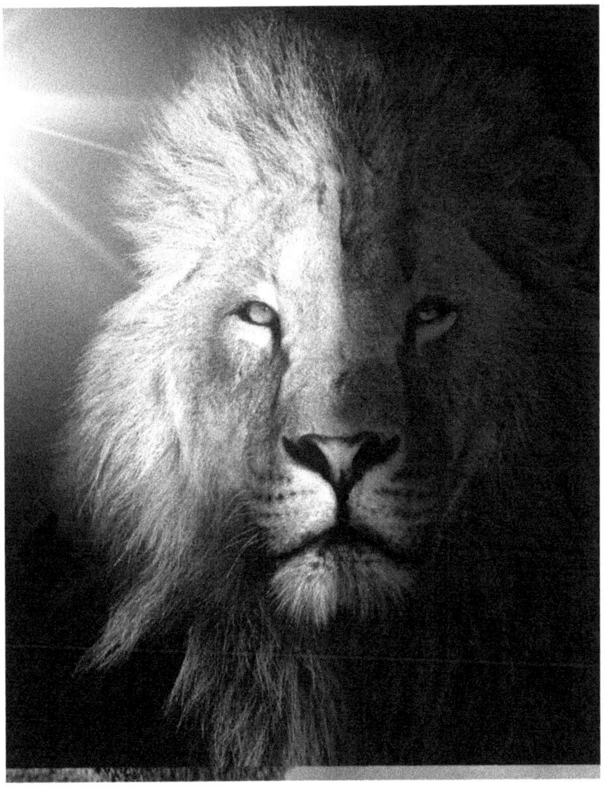

The Desert's Embrace

In vast expanse, a world untamed,
The desert's realm, forever named,
A land of sand, and sun so bright,
A symbol of life, in nature's light.

With dunes so high, and winds so strong,
The desert calls, with a siren's song,
In every step, a chance to roam,
A world of wonder, in every dome.

The desert's heat, in every breath,
A testament to life's sweet breadth,
For in its sands, a life does thrive,
A world of beauty, in every jive.

In tales of old, the desert's lore,
From Bedouin tribes, to Aladdin's score,
A bond of life, forevermore,
In every tale, and every lore.

So let us honor, the desert's grace,
A life's pursuit, in nature's pace,
For in its embrace, we find a part,
Of human's journey, and life's sweet heart.

Embrace the desert, and its might,
A symbol of life, in every sight,
For in its world, we may learn,
Of life's great mysteries, and nature's turn.

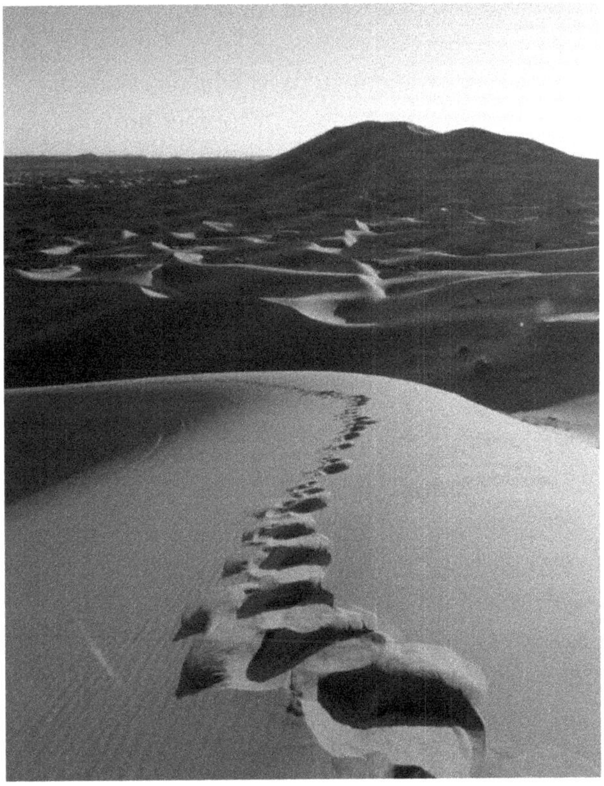

The Journey by Train

On tracks so long, and journeys wide,
The train's great roar, a joyous ride,
In every carriage, a world to find,
A journey of wonder, in every mind.

With chugging engine, and whistle's sound,
The train's great journey, forever bound,
In every stop, a chance to roam,
A world of adventure, in every dome.

The train's great speed, in every mile,
A symbol of life, in every style,
For in its path, a world does thrive,
A world of wonder, in every hive.

In tales of old, the train's lore,
From Orient Express to Hogwarts' door,
A bond of journeys, forevermore,
In every tale, and every lore.

So let us honor, the train's great ride,
A life's pursuit, in every stride,
For in its journey, we find a part,
Of human's travel, and life's sweet art.

Embrace the train, and its power,
A symbol of life, in every hour,
For in its journey, we may learn,
Of life's great mysteries, and travel's turn.

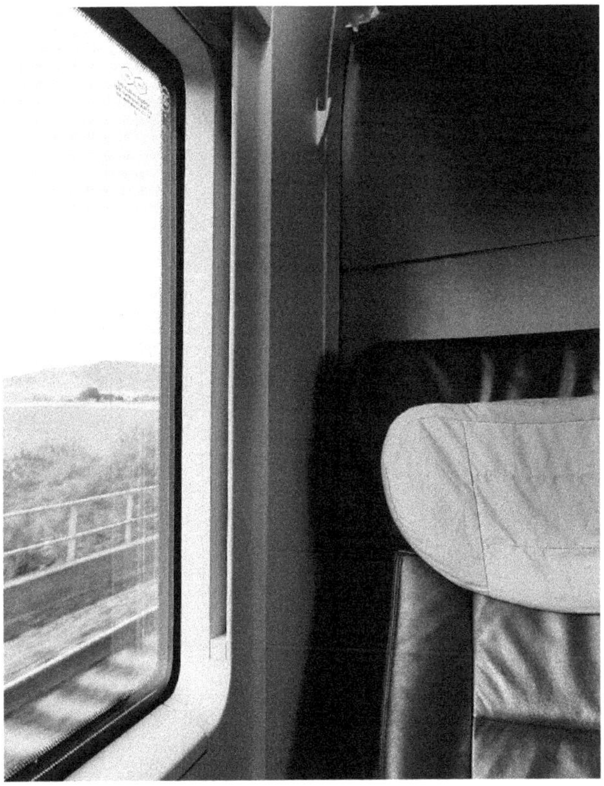

DISCLAIMER AND COPYRIGHT

© Copyright 2023 - *Rhyme O'Matic*

The author has made necessary adjustments to each image in this photo book in order to tailor the photos to the project's requirements. The photo book consists of photographs taken by professional and amateur photographers, with the author of the book holding rights only to the written content and overall idea. Therefore, reproduction of the photos is strictly prohibited, unless authorized by the photographer or by websites that hold the rights to the images. As a result, most of the photos used in this book are not free to use, and the author uses them in their project under the Canva Pro license. Even though the photos may have been modified, the original photographers still own the rights to their respective photos. Reproduction or duplication of this book, either electronically or in print, is considered an illegal act. This includes the creation of secondary or tertiary copies of the work or a recorded copy, and is only allowed with the written consent of the author. All additional rights are reserved. The publisher or the original author of this work cannot be held responsible for any difficulties or damages that may occur after reading the information described here. Additionally, the information contained in this book is solely for informational purposes. All trademarks mentioned are used without written consent and cannot be considered an endorsement by the trademark owner.

Milton Keynes UK
Ingram Content Group UK Ltd.
UKHW051943310723
426115UK00009B/386